MELANIA TRUMP BIOGRAPHY NEW BOOK 2024

A Giftable memoir of Family and power

Lily Harris

Copyright © 2024 by Lily Harris

All rights reserved. No part of this publication may be copied, shared, or reproduced in any manner—whether through photocopying, recording, digital transmission, or any other mechanical or electronic means—without prior written consent from the publisher, except for brief excerpts used in reviews or permitted under applicable copyright laws.

This book is a non-fiction work created for informational and educational purposes. While every effort has been made to ensure the content is accurate and reliable, neither the author nor the publisher accepts liability for any errors, omissions, or varying interpretations of the material presented.

Disclaimer

This publication is an independent, unauthorized non-fiction work and is not affiliated with, endorsed by, or officially connected to Melania Trump, the Trump family, or any related organizations. The information provided is based on thorough research from publicly available sources, combined with the author's analysis and perspectives.

The author and publisher make no guarantees about the accuracy, completeness, or reliability of the information contained in this book. Readers are encouraged to exercise their own judgment when interpreting its contents.

Any similarities to individuals, living or deceased—aside from Melania Trump—are purely coincidental. This book is not intended to damage the reputation, defame, or disparage any person or entity.

All trademarks, product names, and logos referenced remain the property of their respective owners and are mentioned without any implication of sponsorship or endorsement.

Table of Contents

Introduction..7
1. Humble Beginnings in Slovenia.......... 9
3. Meeting Donald Trump: A Love Story.. 20
4. Life as First Lady............................ 27
5. Public Persona vs. Private Life........ 38
6. Beyond the White House................. 46
7. Conclusion: The Enigma of Melania Trump.. 53

A Remarkable Journey

Introduction

Melania Trump, the wife of the 45th President of the United States, Donald Trump, has captivated the world with her intriguing blend of elegance, mystery, and resilience. Originally from Slovenia, she rose to fame as a successful international model before stepping into the global spotlight as First Lady. Known for her poised demeanor and rare public appearances, Melania became a figure of fascination for many. Her life is one of contrasts—she's both admired for her grace and criticized for her silence on key political issues. Despite the scrutiny, Melania's journey from a small town in Eastern Europe to the White House continues to spark curiosity, making her one of the most enigmatic public figures of the 21st century.

1. Humble Beginnings in Slovenia

Melania Trump was born Melania Knauss in Sevnica, a small town nestled along the banks of the Sava River in Slovenia. Growing up in a communist-era Yugoslavia, her early life was shaped by a blend of simplicity and determination. Her father, Viktor Knauss, was a car dealer, and her mother, Amalija, worked as a patternmaker. They instilled in her strong values of hard work, discipline, and the importance of education.

Sevnica, with its picturesque countryside and close-knit community, provided a backdrop of stability during her childhood. Though the country was under political constraints, Melania's parents emphasized the pursuit of personal goals, fostering a sense of independence and ambition in their daughter. From a young age, Melania was drawn to the arts, particularly modeling, which became her passion as she navigated her teenage years. Her upbringing, rooted in traditional Slovenian values, laid the foundation for the poised and focused woman who would one day step onto the world stage.

Melania Trump's academic journey was marked by a strong focus on both education and personal development. She attended the Secondary School of Design and Photography in Ljubljana, Slovenia, where she honed her creative skills and cultivated an interest in the arts. Her early ambitions were not just confined to academics; she aspired to model, and this aspiration gradually took precedence as she entered her late teens.

Although Melania was academically inclined, excelling in languages and arts, her dreams of becoming a successful model began to take shape as she participated in local modeling competitions. Driven by a desire to explore the world beyond Slovenia, she learned several languages, including English, which would later prove essential in her international modeling career.

Her determination to succeed pushed her to pursue modeling full-time after finishing high school, marking the beginning of a career that would lead her to international fame. This transition from academia to the fashion world was fueled by her ambition, discipline, and the solid foundation of values instilled by her family, preparing her for the global stage she would eventually dominate.

2. From Model to Icon

Melania Trump's entry into the modeling industry began at the age of 16 when she caught the attention of a photographer at a fashion show in Ljubljana. This moment marked the start of her journey toward international success. With her striking beauty, tall stature, and poise, she quickly rose through the ranks of the European modeling scene. Her big break came when she signed with a renowned modeling agency in Milan, Italy, and later moved to Paris, where she graced the covers of magazines and appeared in high-profile campaigns.

Her career took a significant leap when she relocated to New York City in 1996, where she signed with the prestigious modeling agency, Wilhelmina Models. It was in New York that Melania's global recognition skyrocketed, as she appeared in major advertisements for brands like Chanel, Rolex, and Fendi. Her presence in top fashion publications such as Vogue and

Harper's Bazaar solidified her status as a sought-after model.

Known for her sophisticated look and refined elegance, Melania became one of the most recognized models of her time, even earning accolades for her professional demeanor and timeless beauty. Her success in the competitive world of fashion was a testament to her ambition, resilience, and dedication to her craft. This period of international success set the stage for the next chapter of her life—one that would transcend the fashion world and lead her to the global stage as First Lady of the United States.

Melania Trump's modeling career was marked by several key milestones that not only shaped her professional trajectory but also influenced her perspective on success, independence, and self-presentation.

One of the earliest milestones was her move to New York in 1996, where she signed with

Wilhelmina Models. This decision was pivotal in shaping her career, as it propelled her into the heart of the global fashion industry. It was here that Melania began to develop a sense of confidence and a deeper understanding of the cultural nuances of the industry. She learned the importance of branding and the power of cultivating a public image—skills that would later serve her in her role as First Lady.

In 2001, Melania became a U.S. citizen, cementing her place in America and expanding her professional opportunities. That same year, she appeared on the cover of Vogue and in several high-profile campaigns, solidifying her status as an international model. Her successful transition from European to American markets taught her the value of adaptability and perseverance in an ever-changing world.

Another key milestone was her marriage to Donald Trump in 2005. While her career was already flourishing, becoming part of the Trump family added a new layer to her public persona. It shaped her understanding of the complexities of wealth, power, and media scrutiny.

These milestones, along with her experiences working with elite brands and navigating both the public and private realms, shaped Melania's worldview. She developed a keen sense of discretion, the importance of maintaining personal boundaries, and the value of hard work. These lessons played a pivotal role in her approach to life in the White House, where her focus remained on supporting her family while remaining steadfast in her quiet yet effective public role.

3. Meeting Donald Trump: A Love Story

Melania Trump first met Donald Trump in 1998 at a fashion event in New York City. At the time, Melania was an established model, and Donald was a well-known real estate mogul. According to both, their first encounter was marked by a sense of instant attraction, but it was far from love at first sight. Donald, known for his larger-than-life persona, was immediately struck by Melania's beauty, while she was initially cautious and uninterested in getting involved with someone so publicly prominent.

Their relationship began to evolve after several months of courtship. Melania, who had kept her personal life relatively private, was drawn to Donald's ambition and charm. Meanwhile, Donald admired her intellect, independence, and the way she carried herself, both in private and in the public eye. They shared a common understanding of ambition, with both driven by personal success and a desire to remain in control of their lives.

In 2004, after several years of dating, Donald proposed to Melania with a 15-carat diamond ring, and they married the following year in a lavish ceremony at his Mar-a-Lago estate in Palm Beach, Florida. Their wedding was a media spectacle, attended by celebrities and political figures, and it solidified their partnership in the public eye.

Over the years, their relationship has been one of mutual support, with Melania remaining a private figure while Donald's career and political aspirations took center stage. Despite the challenges and media scrutiny that came with Donald's rise to the presidency, Melania has consistently stood by his side, becoming a steadfast partner in his personal and political journey. Their relationship has evolved from a cautious beginning to one rooted in shared goals, understanding, and a deep, enduring bond.

Melania Trump's marriage to Donald Trump in 2005 marked the beginning of her formal entry into the Trump family and the broader public eye. The couple's wedding was a highly publicized affair, featuring a grand ceremony at Donald's Mar-a-Lago estate in Palm Beach, Florida, which further solidified their place in high society. Despite the lavish celebration, Melania remained a more private and reserved figure, in contrast to Donald's media-savvy, larger-than-life persona.

As part of the Trump dynasty, Melania's life quickly intertwined with the complexities of being married to one of the most influential and controversial figures in America. She embraced her new role with grace, navigating the responsibilities of family life while managing her own career. Melania and Donald's son, Barron, was born in 2006, and his arrival added a new dynamic to their family life. Melania took a hands-on approach to motherhood, often keeping Barron out of the media spotlight during his early years, reflecting her desire to maintain a sense of normalcy and privacy for him.

Over time, Melania became more integrated into the Trump family's business empire, participating in events and public appearances alongside Donald. While she maintained a relatively low profile in comparison to her husband's highly public career, she developed a distinctive presence, marked by her elegance and poised demeanor. She also took on a more public role as the Trump family expanded their influence, with Melania standing by Donald through his business endeavors and eventual presidential campaign.

Her role within the Trump dynasty expanded significantly when Donald ran for president in 2016. As First Lady, Melania became not only a wife and mother but also a global ambassador for the Trump brand. Her marriage to Donald, though marked by moments of public controversy and scrutiny, ultimately positioned her as a central figure in the family's legacy. Through it all, Melania has remained steadfast in her commitment to her family and her own values, demonstrating resilience and a quiet strength as she navigated the complexities of her new life within the Trump dynasty.

4. Life as First Lady

Melania Trump's transition into the role of First Lady of the United States in January 2017 was a momentous shift in her life. As a former model and businesswoman, she had already experienced the pressures of public attention, but this new role thrust her into an entirely different sphere of influence, with its own set of expectations and challenges.

In the early days of her husband's presidential campaign, Melania kept a relatively low profile, focusing on supporting Donald's political ambitions without directly engaging in the political fray herself. However, as the election neared and Donald won, the reality of her position became clear. As First Lady, she would be thrust into the public eye in ways she had never experienced before.

One of her first decisions was to remain in New York City with her son Barron for several months after the inauguration, a decision that sparked public discussion but also highlighted her dedication to maintaining a stable family life. This choice underscored Melania's focus on her son's well-being during the transition, something she continued to prioritize throughout her time in the White House.

As First Lady, Melania embraced a more traditional role, focusing on charitable work, children's issues, and promoting well-being. She launched the Be Best initiative in 2018, aimed at combating cyberbullying, supporting children's health, and encouraging positive social and emotional development. The initiative reflected her personal interests and values, though it also drew mixed reactions from the public.

Throughout her tenure, Melania navigated the challenges of balancing her private nature with the demands of being First Lady. She chose to keep a relatively low public profile compared to her predecessors, yet her elegance and style made her a fashion icon. While she was often scrutinized for her silence on political matters, Melania remained focused on her causes, asserting that her role was to support her husband while also making a positive impact on society in her own way. Her time as First Lady was marked by a distinct quiet strength, as she managed her duties with grace while prioritizing her family and personal values.

As First Lady of the United States, Melania Trump initiated several key programs aimed at addressing issues she felt passionate about, with her most prominent initiative being Be Best. Launched in May 2018, Be Best was a broad, three-pillar campaign focused on promoting the well-being of children, advocating against cyberbullying, and encouraging responsible online behavior. The initiative sought to create a positive environment for children to grow up in, highlighting the importance of emotional and social development.

One of the core components of Be Best was its emphasis on combating cyberbullying, an issue Melania personally felt strongly about. She advocated for kindness, respect, and positive online interactions, making the case that young people should be guided in navigating the digital world safely. While her stance on cyberbullying was met with mixed reactions, given the challenges her husband faced in his own use of social media, it remained one of the central tenets of her campaign.

In addition to cyberbullying, Be Best addressed childhood wellness, including the importance of healthy living and mental health. Melania promoted the need for a supportive and safe environment for children, both at home and in schools, by collaborating with healthcare organizations and various nonprofits to raise awareness about mental health challenges that children face today. She also encouraged the importance of early childhood education, advocating for programs that support young minds in their formative years.

Through Be Best, Melania aimed to bring attention to these pressing issues, often working behind the scenes with organizations, hospitals, and schools to support initiatives aligned with her campaign. Despite facing some criticism, her efforts in this area reflected a genuine desire to make a positive impact on the next generation and support children in overcoming the unique challenges they face in today's digital age.

Melania Trump's tenure as First Lady was marked by both challenges and highlights, as she navigated the complexities of her public role while maintaining her personal values.

Challenges:
One of the most significant challenges Melania faced was the constant media

scrutiny, especially as it related to her relationship with her husband, President Donald Trump. While she kept a relatively low profile compared to previous First Ladies, her every move was still closely watched and often criticized. Her silence on certain political issues, particularly in the highly polarized climate of her husband's presidency, led to questions about her stance on important matters, with some critics accusing her of being disengaged or indifferent.

Additionally, the ongoing public attention on her marriage and personal life created a difficult balance for Melania. The media's focus on her appearance, behavior, and even her choice to remain in New York for several months after the inauguration was often seen as an effort to undermine her. Despite these challenges, Melania chose to remain focused on her causes, avoiding the political spotlight while dedicating herself to her role as First Lady.

Highlights:
Despite the challenges, there were several notable successes during Melania's time in the White House. The Be Best campaign, which focused on childhood well-being, cyberbullying prevention, and education, became one of her most recognizable initiatives. Though controversial at times, it allowed her to champion causes that resonated with many, particularly those concerned with children's mental health and digital safety.

Her role as a fashion icon was another highlight. Known for her impeccable style, Melania made several appearances in high-profile outfits that garnered attention both in the U.S. and abroad. She was frequently praised for her elegance and poise, particularly during her travels to meet foreign leaders. Her fashion choices became a subject of admiration, further solidifying her position as one of the most recognizable women in the world.

Internationally, Melania was often praised for her diplomacy, particularly during her visits to countries like Africa and Asia. Her trips were seen as opportunities to build bridges and support causes related to children's health and education, further highlighting her commitment to her initiatives. Her ability to navigate these high-stakes diplomatic situations with grace was a testament to her growing role as a global ambassador.

Through both challenges and successes, Melania Trump's tenure as First Lady demonstrated her resilience and commitment to her personal agenda, while also showcasing the unique nature of her time in the White House.

5. Public Persona vs. Private Life

Melania Trump's time as First Lady was defined by a distinct balance between her reserved, private nature and the public responsibilities that came with her position. Unlike many of her predecessors, who embraced the role of First Lady with frequent public appearances and outspoken advocacy, Melania opted for a more reserved approach, choosing to remain largely out of the spotlight unless necessary. This decision was both a personal preference and a strategic one, as she maintained a sense of privacy amidst the intense media scrutiny.

Her reserved nature was evident in her reluctance to publicly comment on many political issues, especially those surrounding her husband's presidency. While other First Ladies were often vocal in their support or opposition to policies, Melania rarely expressed strong political opinions, preferring to focus on her initiatives, particularly those related to children's well-being and mental health. This choice led to mixed reactions from the public, some appreciating her focus on positive causes while others criticized her silence on contentious issues.

Despite her personal inclination toward privacy, Melania still understood the importance of her public duties. She appeared at numerous state functions, both domestically and internationally, where her composed demeanor and diplomatic presence were lauded. Her public responsibilities also included engaging in charity work, championing the Be Best campaign, and representing the United States at various international events, where she balanced her natural reticence with a polished professionalism.

Her ability to navigate this balance between private life and public duty was also reflected in her approach to social media. While her husband often dominated the online space, Melania's social media presence remained more controlled and selective, focusing on her initiatives and family.

Ultimately, Melania's reserved nature became a defining feature of her tenure as First Lady. While it occasionally led to criticisms of her perceived aloofness, it also allowed her to carve out a role that was uniquely her own—one that emphasized quiet strength, discretion, and a dedication to her causes, without the need for constant public visibility.

Melania Trump's values and personality reflect a combination of independence, resilience, and a strong sense of privacy. Raised in Sevnica, Slovenia, her upbringing emphasized the importance of hard work, family, and a commitment to personal success. These foundational values shaped the woman who would later navigate the complexities of being married to one of the most prominent figures in the world.

Her personality is often described as reserved, calm, and measured. While she shied away from the spotlight in comparison to other First Ladies, Melania exuded an elegance and dignity that became her trademark. Her preference for a more private, less public-facing role in the White House demonstrated her desire to remain grounded despite the immense attention placed on her. This quality of privacy, which she has maintained throughout her life, is a key part of her identity. Melania often kept her personal beliefs and feelings close to her chest, preferring to show support through actions rather than words.

One of the defining aspects of Melania's character is her ability to manage public scrutiny. Given her status as First Lady and her marriage to Donald Trump, she has faced intense media coverage and criticism. Yet, Melania has consistently shown resilience in handling these pressures. She rarely responded to negative media coverage directly, instead choosing to focus on her initiatives, particularly her Be Best campaign, which she used as a platform to promote positive causes like children's well-being and cyberbullying prevention.

Her ability to maintain composure amidst public scrutiny has often been attributed to her focus on her values. Melania's sense of purpose, whether it's supporting her family or advocating for the causes she cares about, has allowed her to rise above the negative aspects of fame. She doesn't seek validation from the public or media, which is in contrast to the constant public attention her husband attracted. Instead, she relies on her inner strength, maintaining a sense of control over her image and actions.

In essence, Melania Trump's values, personality, and management of public scrutiny reflect a woman who is both independent and strategic. While she may have faced criticism or misinterpretations along the way, her ability to stay focused on her personal goals and maintain a sense of dignity throughout her public life has been one of her defining traits.

6. Beyond the White House

After the presidency, Melania Trump has continued to maintain a relatively low profile, staying out of the public eye while also pursuing a few personal and professional projects. True to her reserved nature, she has largely avoided the intense media scrutiny that often follows former First Ladies, instead focusing on her family and maintaining her privacy. However, she has not entirely stepped away from the public sphere, quietly continuing some of her initiatives and personal endeavors.

One of Melania's ongoing projects is her work with Be Best, the campaign she launched during her time in the White House to promote children's well-being, combat cyberbullying, and encourage kindness in the digital world. While she has scaled back her public involvement in the initiative since leaving office, Melania has expressed a commitment to continuing her work in these areas. She remains involved in supporting organizations and causes that align with Be Best, though her activities in this regard are often less visible than during her time in the White House.

Melania has also shown interest in re-engaging with the business world, particularly through her brand and public speaking engagements. She has expressed a desire to pursue projects that allow her to influence social causes, particularly those related to children's health, education, and online safety.

Additionally, there have been rumors and reports suggesting that Melania could be exploring writing a book, possibly reflecting on her experiences as First Lady or sharing her perspectives on life after the White House. However, these plans have not yet materialized into concrete public announcements, and her career post-presidency appears to be focused more on maintaining a private life, raising her son Barron, and supporting her husband's political ventures.

In sum, life after the presidency has seen Melania Trump continue to pursue a quiet, purposeful existence while remaining committed to the causes she cares about. She has focused on maintaining her family's privacy, supporting ongoing initiatives from behind the scenes, and exploring opportunities that align with her personal values.

Melania Trump's legacy as First Lady is shaped by her distinct approach to the role, which contrasted with the more public-facing and outspoken positions of her predecessors. While she was often perceived as a more private and reserved figure, her contributions and legacy are defined by her focus on key causes, particularly those related to children's well-being, online safety, and her support for family and traditional values.

One of her most notable contributions was the Be Best initiative, which aimed to promote children's health, combat cyberbullying, and encourage positive social interactions. While the campaign garnered mixed reactions, its focus on children's mental health and the importance of kindness and respect in the digital age resonated with many. Through Be Best, Melania highlighted the growing concerns around the negative effects of social media on young people, making it a defining aspect of her time as First Lady.

In addition to her work with Be Best, Melania's legacy includes her diplomatic role on the global stage. Her travels abroad as First Lady—especially her visits to Africa and Asia—were opportunities to build international relationships and bring attention to causes such as education and health. Melania's calm and composed demeanor in these settings helped solidify her reputation as a figure who was dedicated to diplomacy and the well-being of children worldwide.

While Melania's public role was often subdued compared to her husband's, she made a lasting impact through her quiet strength and ability to manage the pressures of being in the spotlight. She demonstrated resilience in the face of criticism, choosing to remain focused on her family and her causes rather than engaging in public disputes. Her ability to maintain a sense of privacy while still fulfilling her role as First Lady set her apart from others in the position.

Her legacy, though understated, will likely be remembered for her commitment to children's causes, her graceful diplomacy, and her unique approach to the First Lady role. By balancing her private life with her public responsibilities, Melania Trump carved out a legacy that speaks to her strength, discretion, and dedication to the values she holds dear.

7. Conclusion: The Enigma of Melania Trump

Melania Trump's impact as First Lady and her enduring fascination lie in the complexity of her persona and her ability to maintain a sense of mystery while fulfilling her role in the public eye. Unlike many of her predecessors, Melania took a more reserved and private approach to her position, which both intrigued and perplexed the public. Her quiet strength, combined with the unique challenges and scrutiny that came with being married to one of the most polarizing figures in American politics, has left a lasting impression on the public consciousness.

Her initiatives, particularly Be Best, while not universally embraced, addressed important issues such as children's mental health, online safety, and bullying—topics that remain highly relevant today. Despite criticism and mixed reactions, Melania's commitment to these causes underscored her desire to make a positive impact, particularly in the realm of child development and well-being. Her focus on these areas, alongside her diplomatic roles during international visits, showcased her desire to contribute to society in ways that aligned with her values, even if she did so without the high-profile advocacy that many might have expected.

The fascination with Melania Trump extends beyond her First Lady tenure and stems from the contrasts between her public persona and private life. As a figure who frequently chose to remain out of the spotlight, she became a subject of speculation and intrigue. The media often focused on her appearance, her marriage, and her ability to navigate the complexities of the Trump presidency, but much of her story remained unspoken, fueling the curiosity about her true personality, beliefs, and ambitions.

Ultimately, Melania's legacy is one of resilience and discretion. While she may not have sought fame or recognition through the traditional channels of public life, her impact as First Lady is undeniable. Her approach to the role, which prioritized her family, her values, and a more private existence, has led to a complex but lasting legacy. The enduring fascination with her story reflects the public's desire to understand not only the woman behind the title but also the strength and conviction that allowed her to manage her public responsibilities while maintaining her personal identity.

Made in United States
Cleveland, OH
29 January 2025